This Book Belongs to

....

HE LIVES

T.S. DOBSON

HE LIVES
COLOR FOR THE SOUL

A Coloring Book of Crosses & Scripture

ISBN-13: 978-1530908332
ISBN-10: 1530908337

Cover and Interior Art by Teresa Scott Dobson

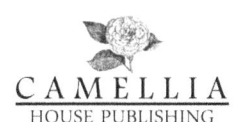

CAMELLIA
HOUSE PUBLISHING

Camellia House Publishing, Century, FL
Printed in the United States of America.

camelliahousepublishing@aol.com

Before You Get Started!

1. Put away all of the worldly distractions around you -- TV, phone, computer, etc. Get alone with God!

2. Take out some color pencils, markers or crayons.

3. Pick a page and go with it. There's no particular order to follow. Let God's Spirit guide you. Practice meditating on God and cast away your worry, stress, fear, and anxiety.

4. When you finish a design, personalize it by signing your name anywhere on the page.

5. Find the Doodle Drawing Pad in the back of the book and color the doodles.

6. Stop when you need a break, then pick it up again later.

7. When finished, if you desire, share your creations with others!

We would love to see any of your finished creations! Send a picture of your art to

camelliahousepublishing@aol.com

(Attach png or jpeg files 10 megs or less per email)

"For God so loved the world, that He gave His only Son, that whoever believes in him should not perish but have eternal life."

John 3:16 NKJV

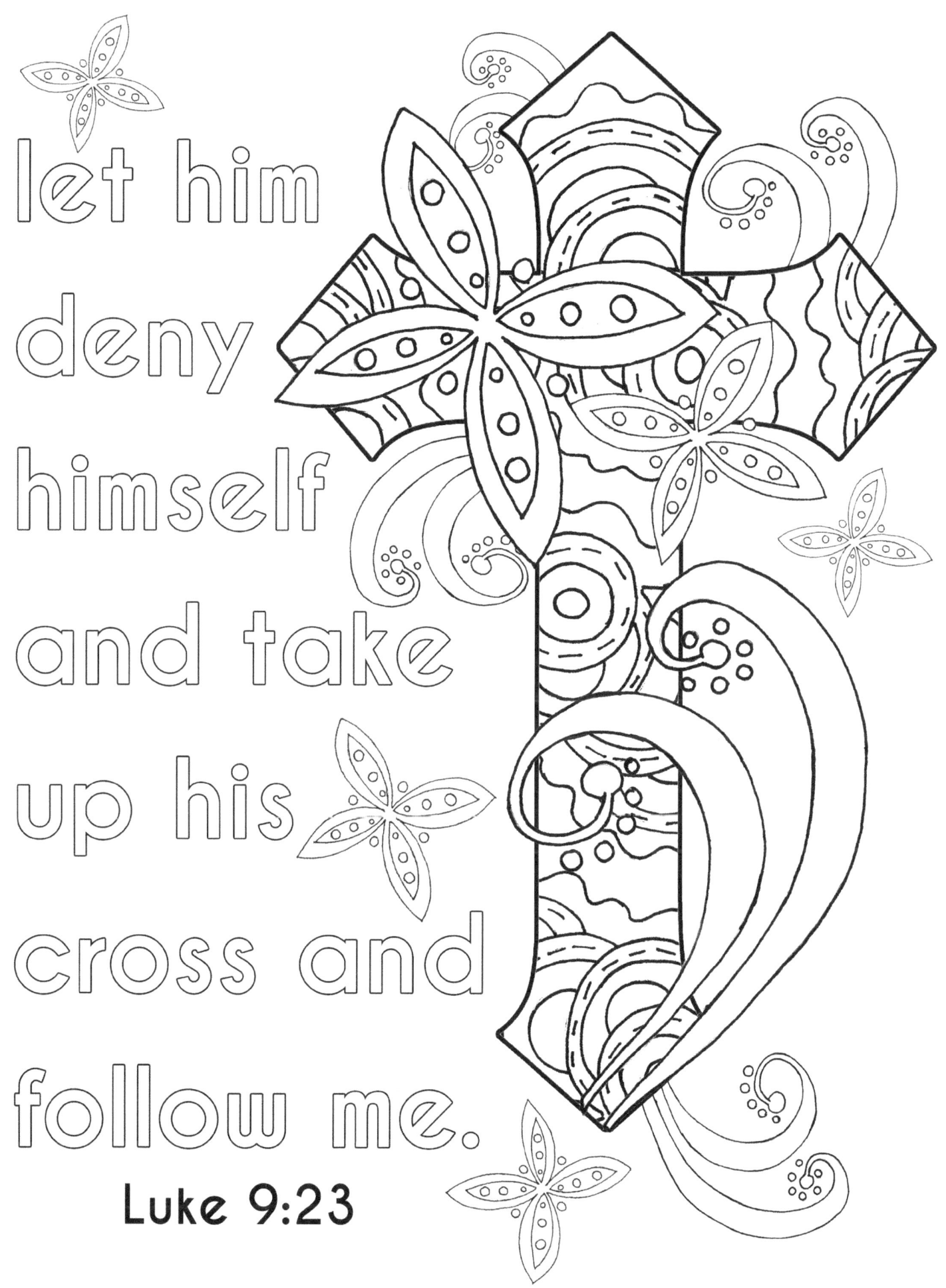

let him
deny
himself
and take
up his
cross and
follow me.
Luke 9:23

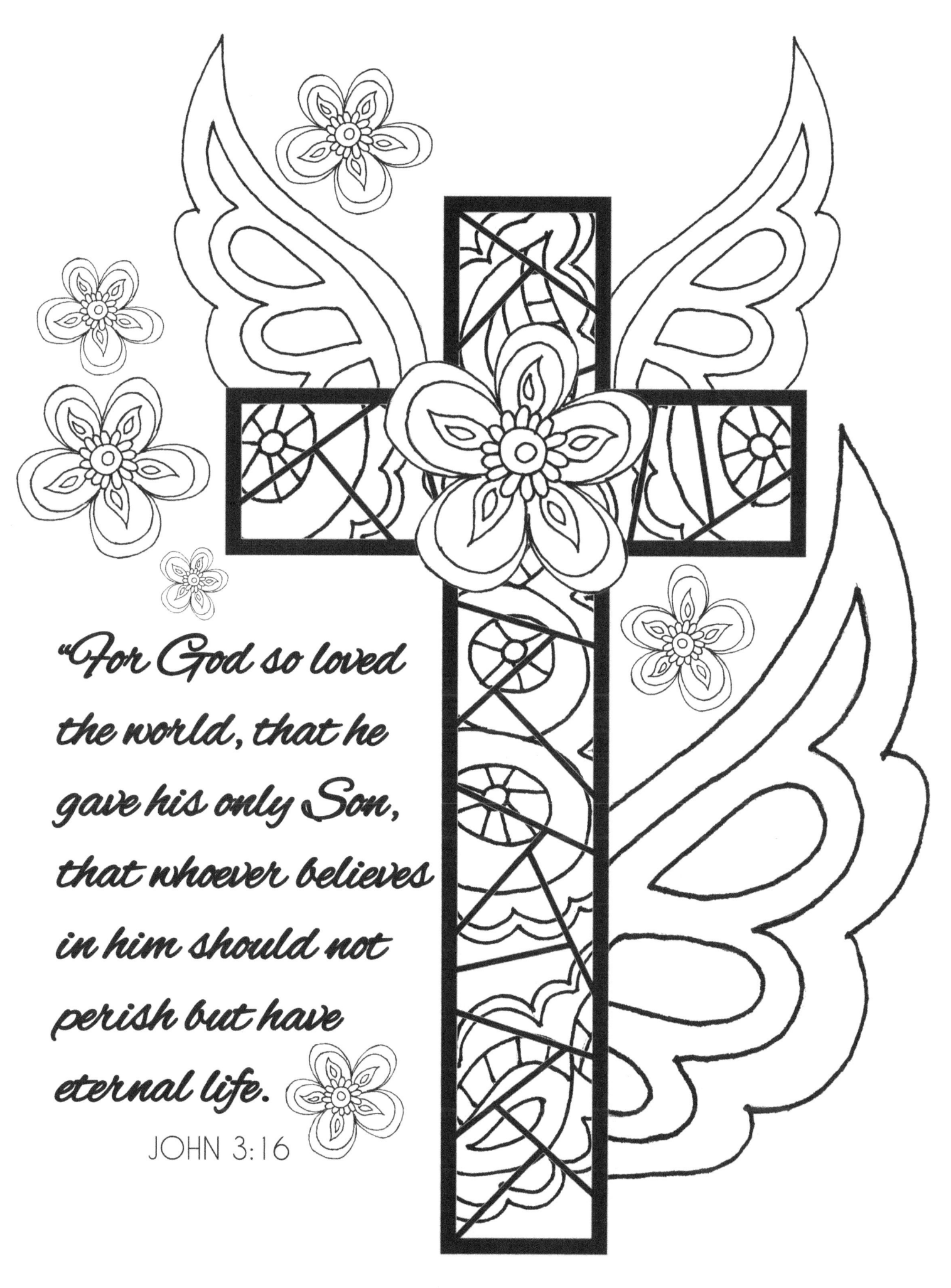

"For God so loved the world, that he gave his only Son, that whoever believes in him should not perish but have eternal life.

JOHN 3:16

But God shows his love for us in that while we were still sinners, Christ died for us.
Romans 5:8

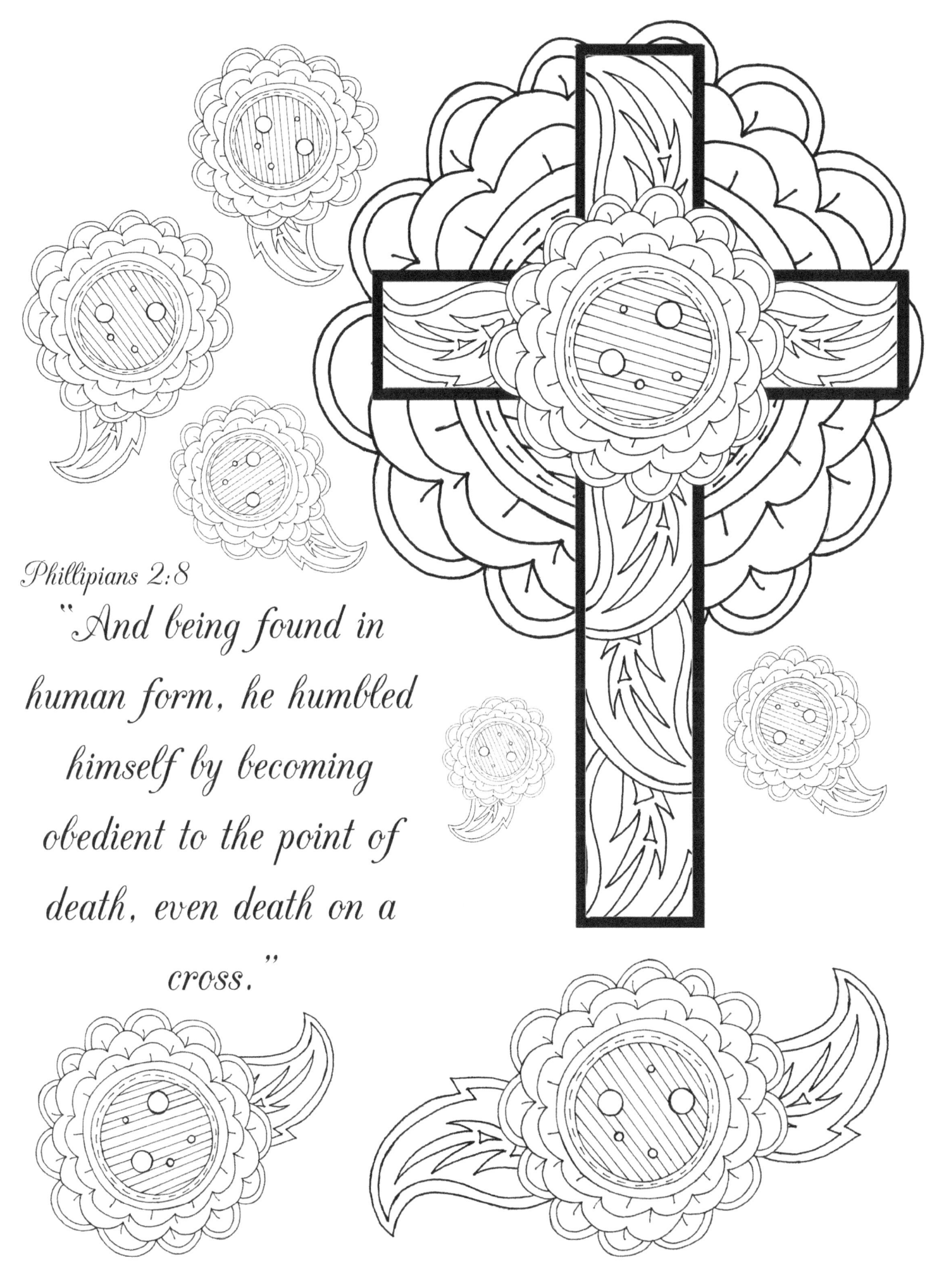

Phillipians 2:8

"And being found in human form, he humbled himself by becoming obedient to the point of death, even death on a cross."

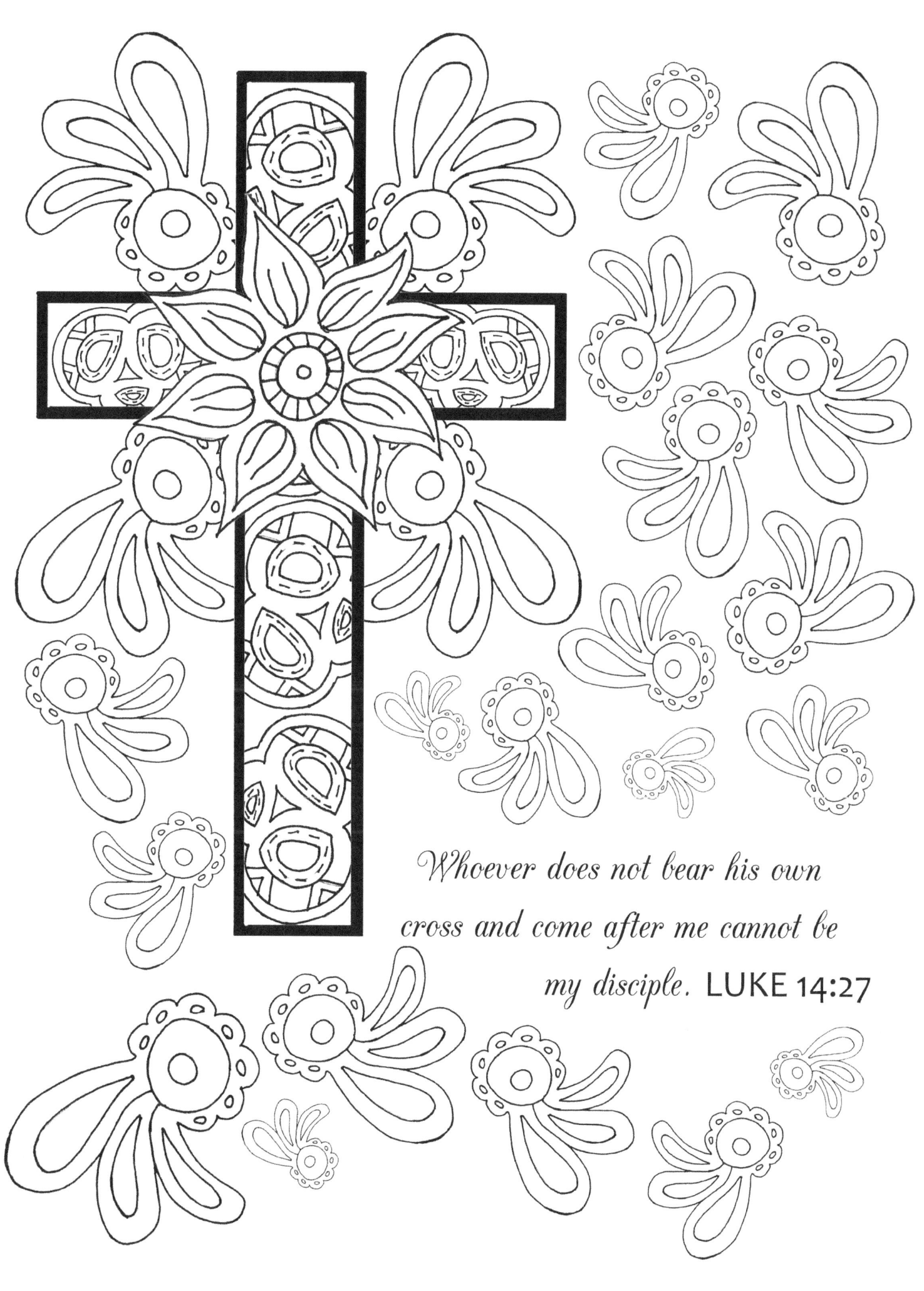

Whoever does not bear his own cross and come after me cannot be my disciple. LUKE 14:27

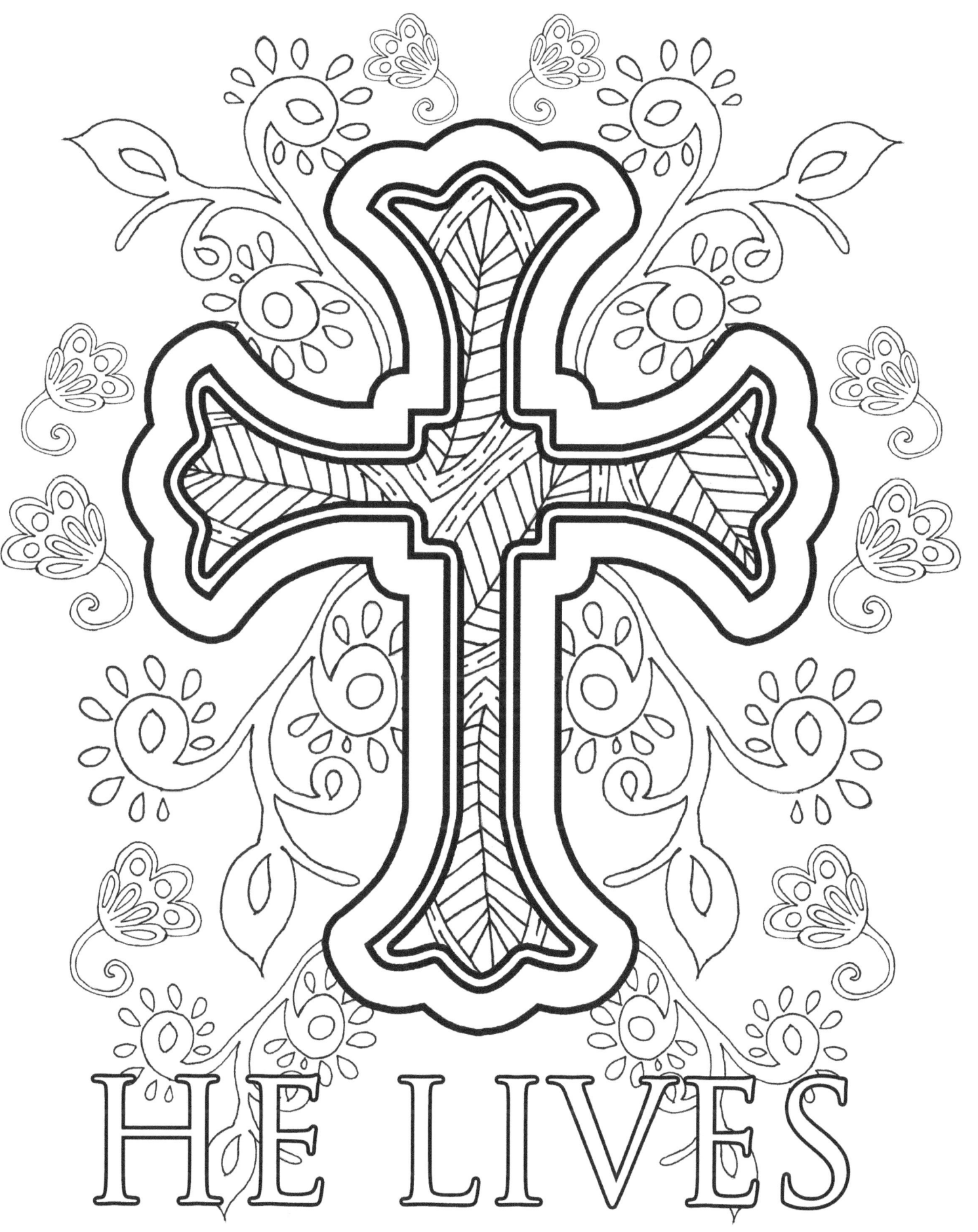

HE LIVES

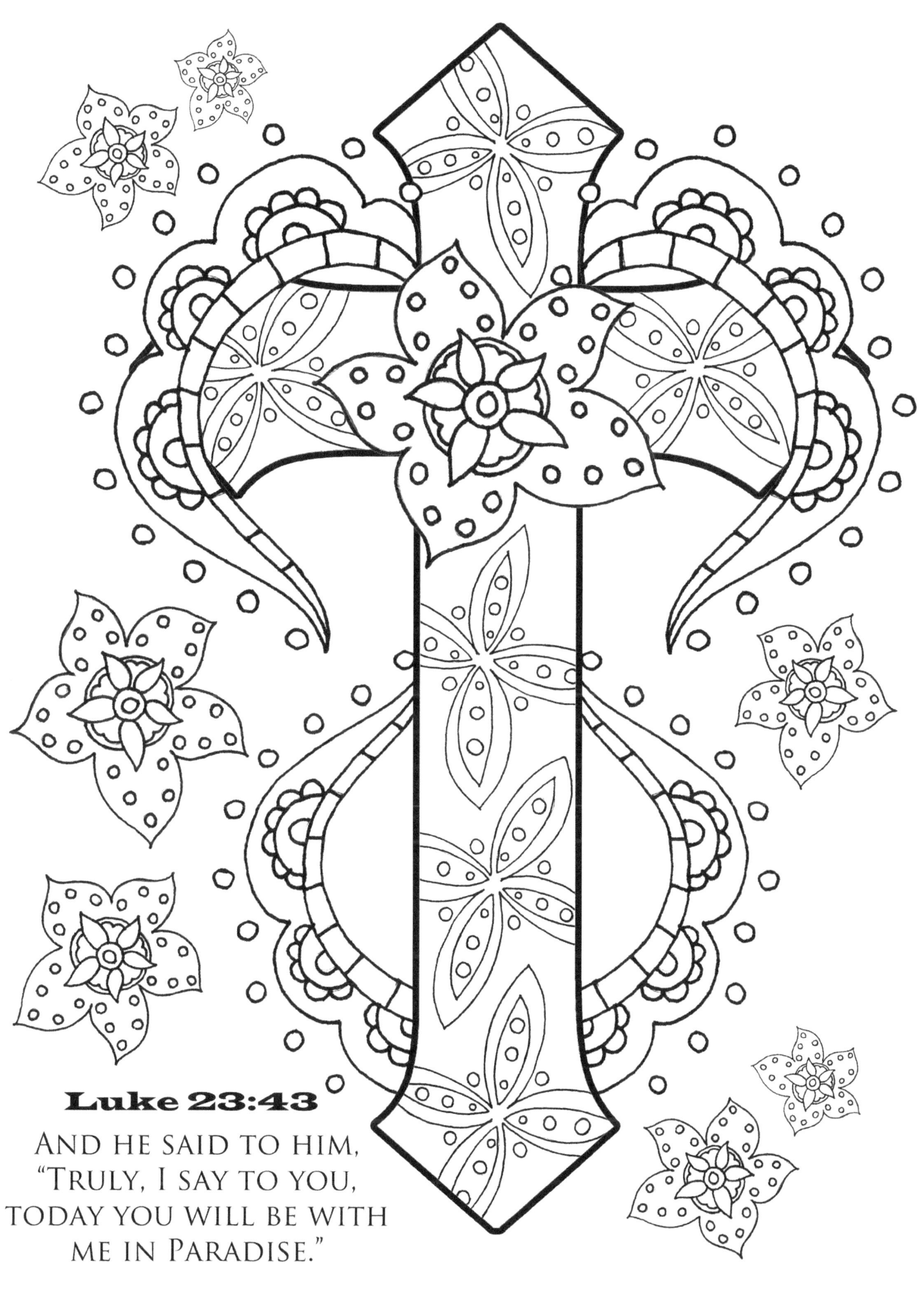

Luke 23:43

AND HE SAID TO HIM,
"TRULY, I SAY TO YOU,
TODAY YOU WILL BE WITH
ME IN PARADISE."

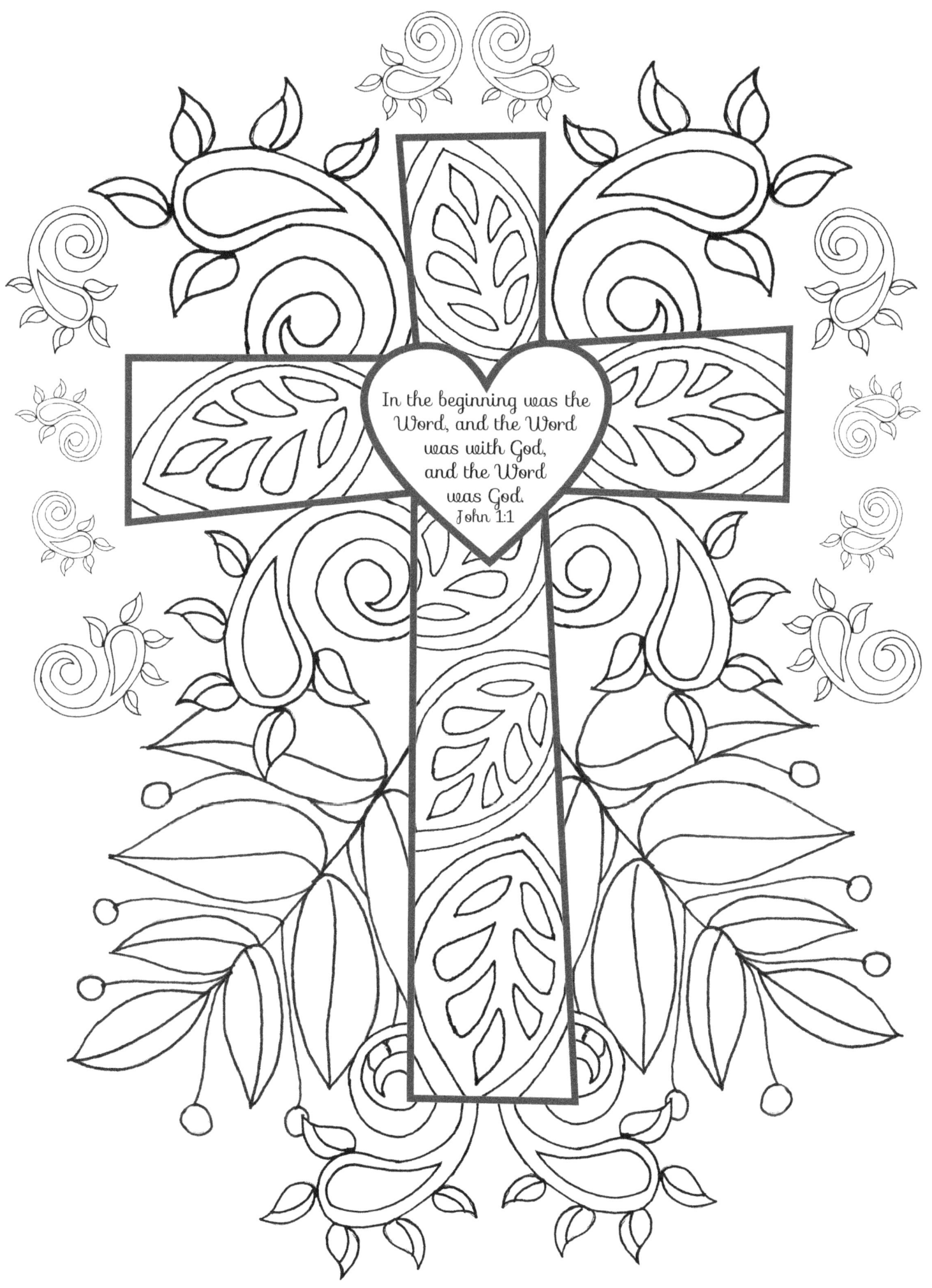

In the beginning was the Word, and the Word was with God, and the Word was God. John 1:1

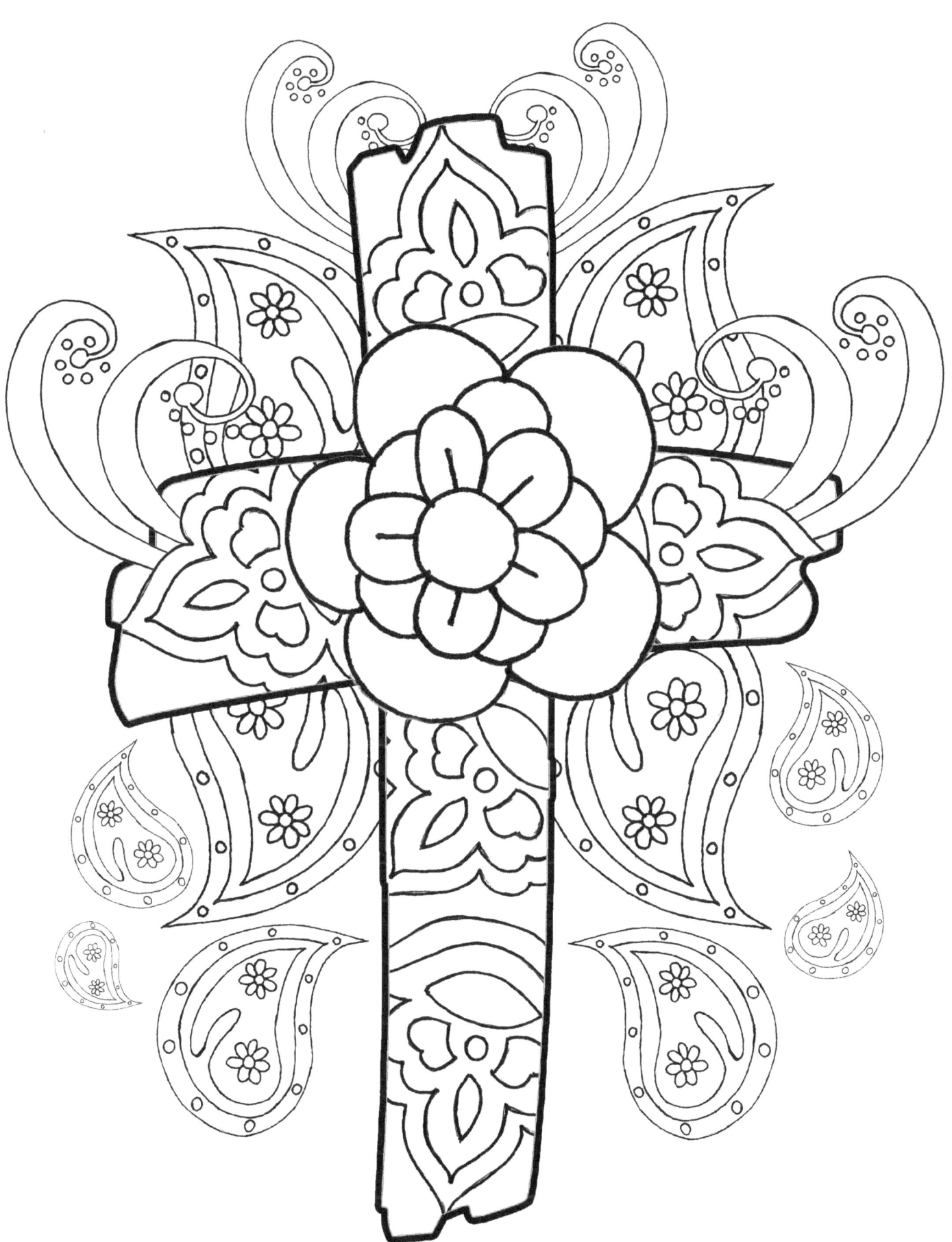

He himself bore our sins in his body on the tree, that we might die
to sin and live to righteousness. By his wounds you have been
healed. 1 Peter 2:24-25

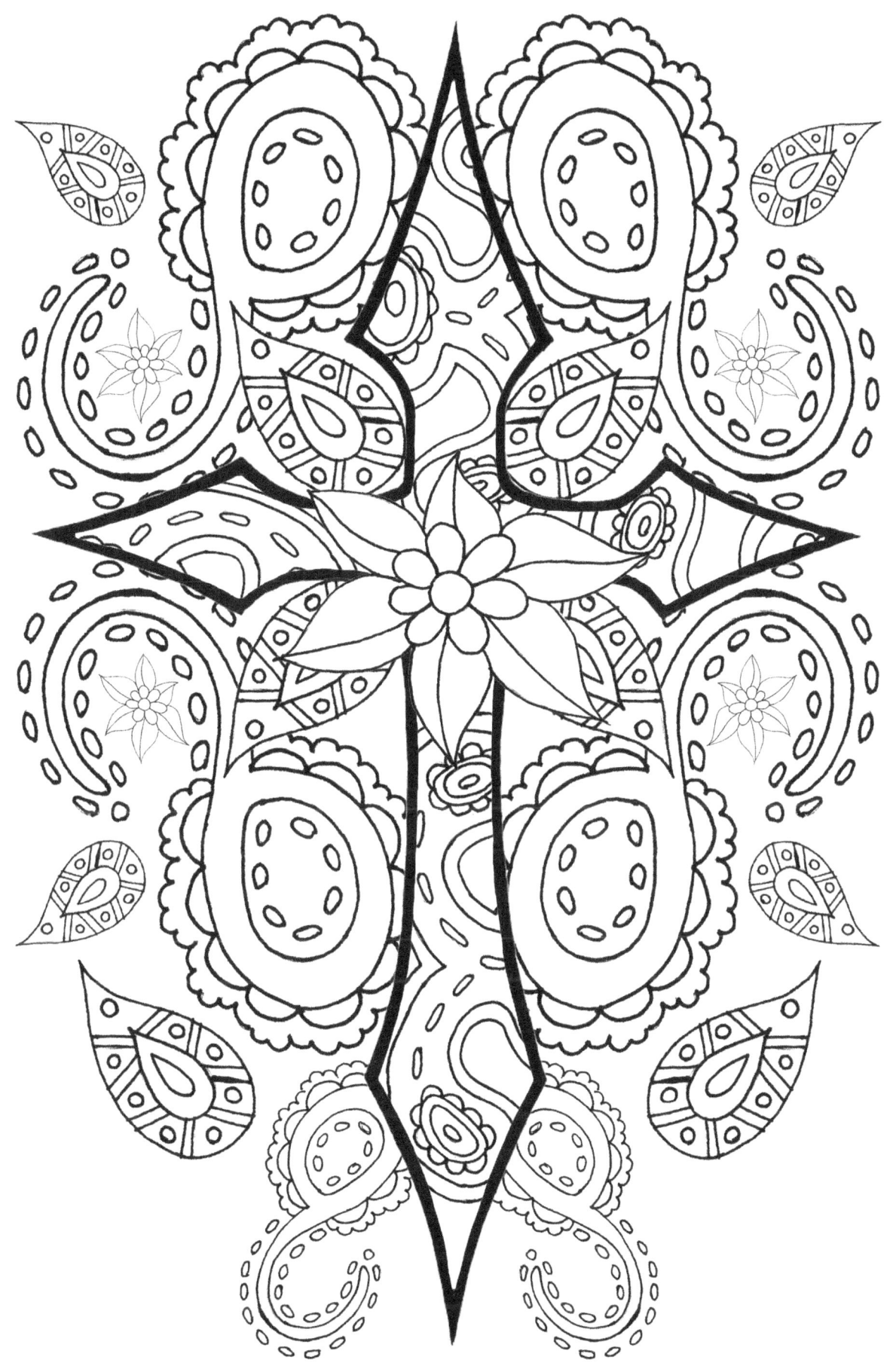

"For the word of the cross is folly to those who are perishing, but to us who are being saved it is the power of God." 1 Corinthians 1:18

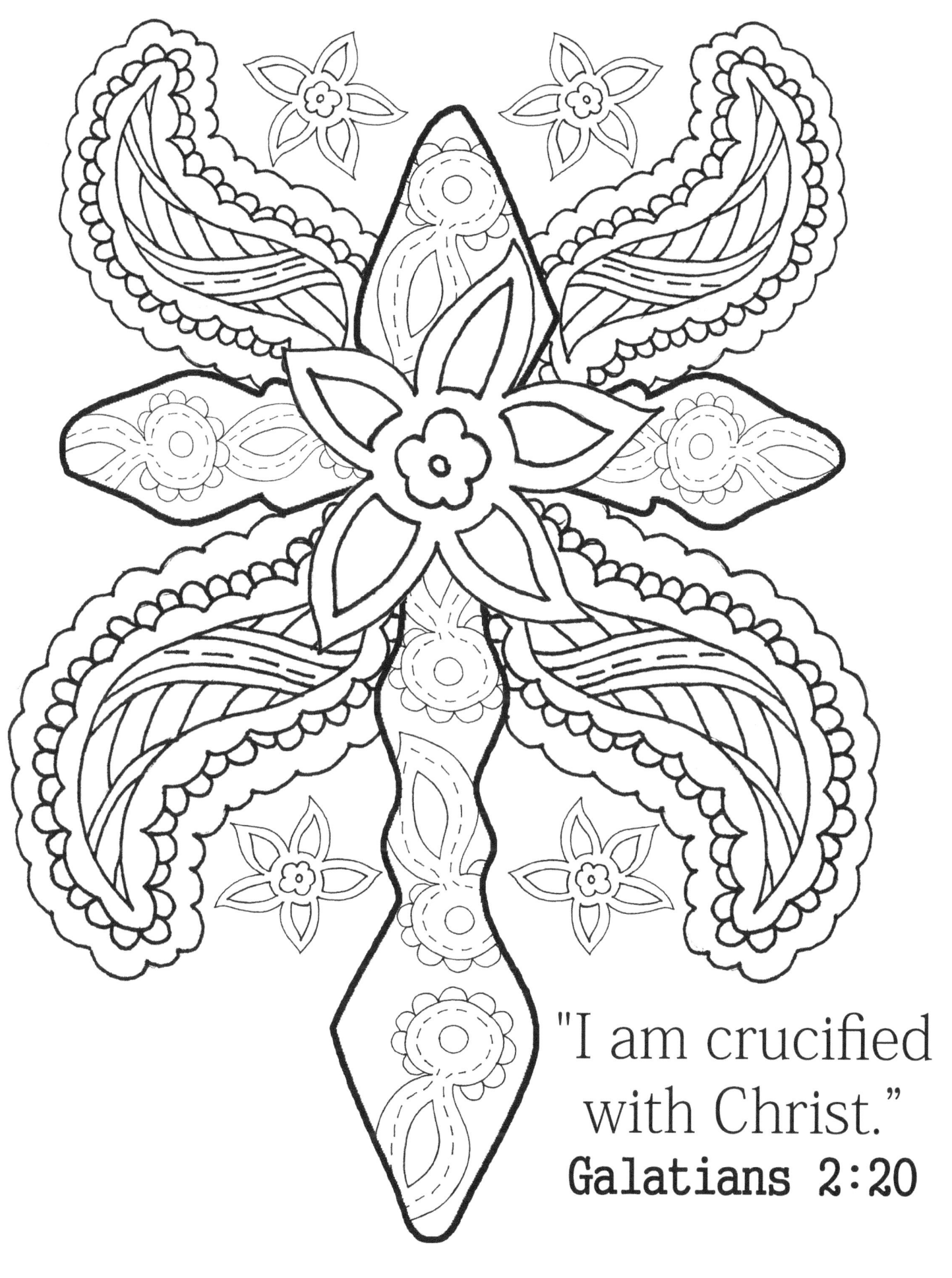

"I am crucified with Christ."
Galatians 2:20

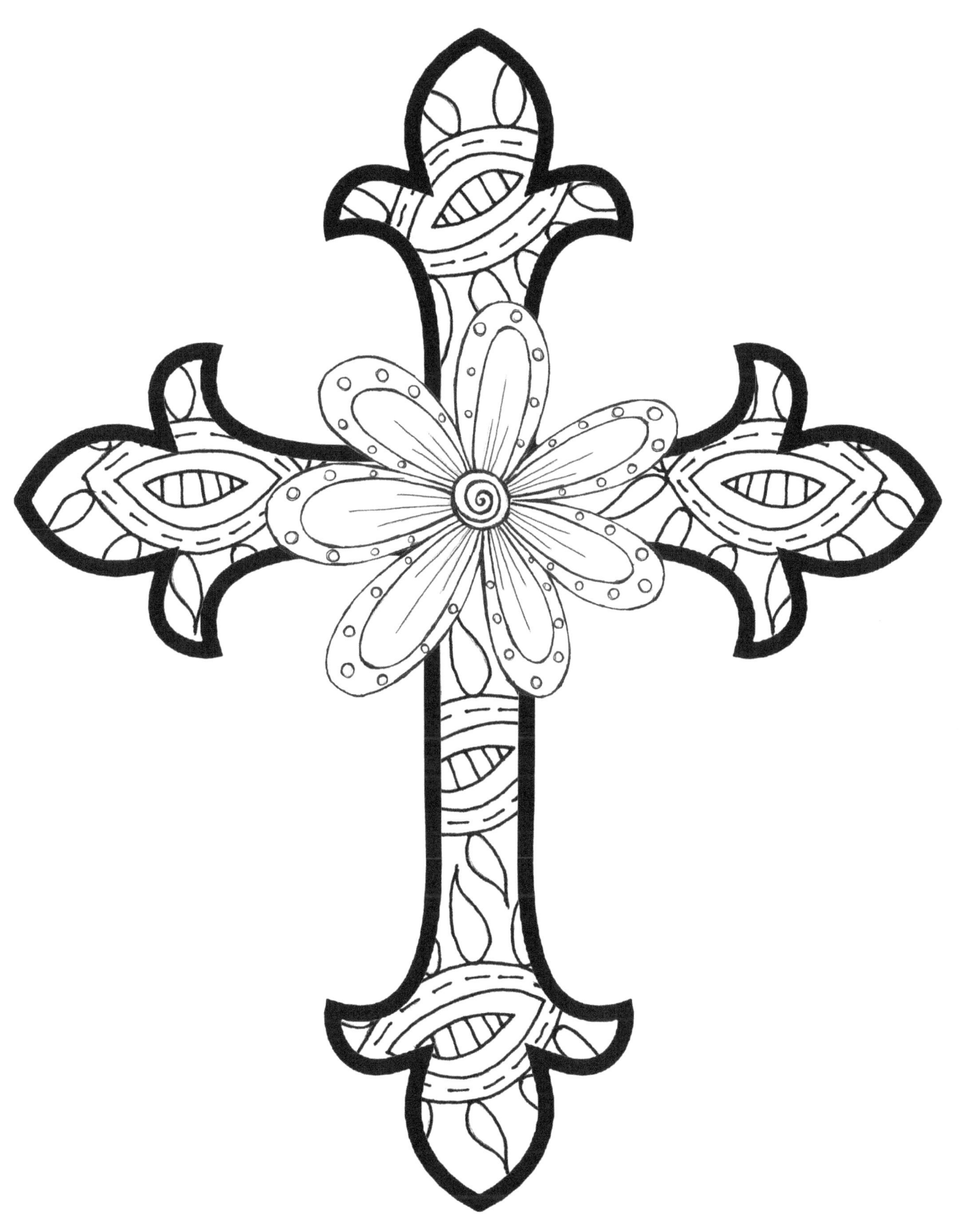

"Father, into Your hands I commit My spirit." LUKE 23:46

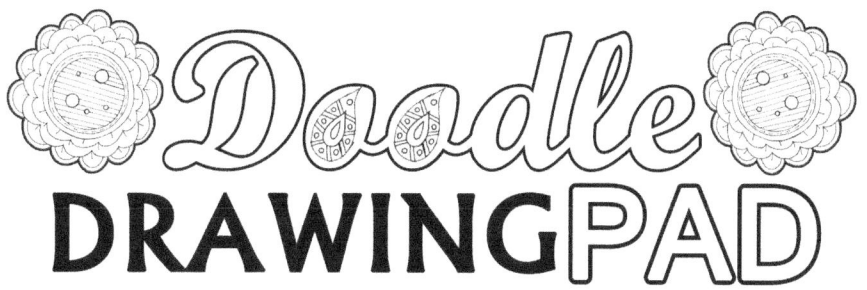

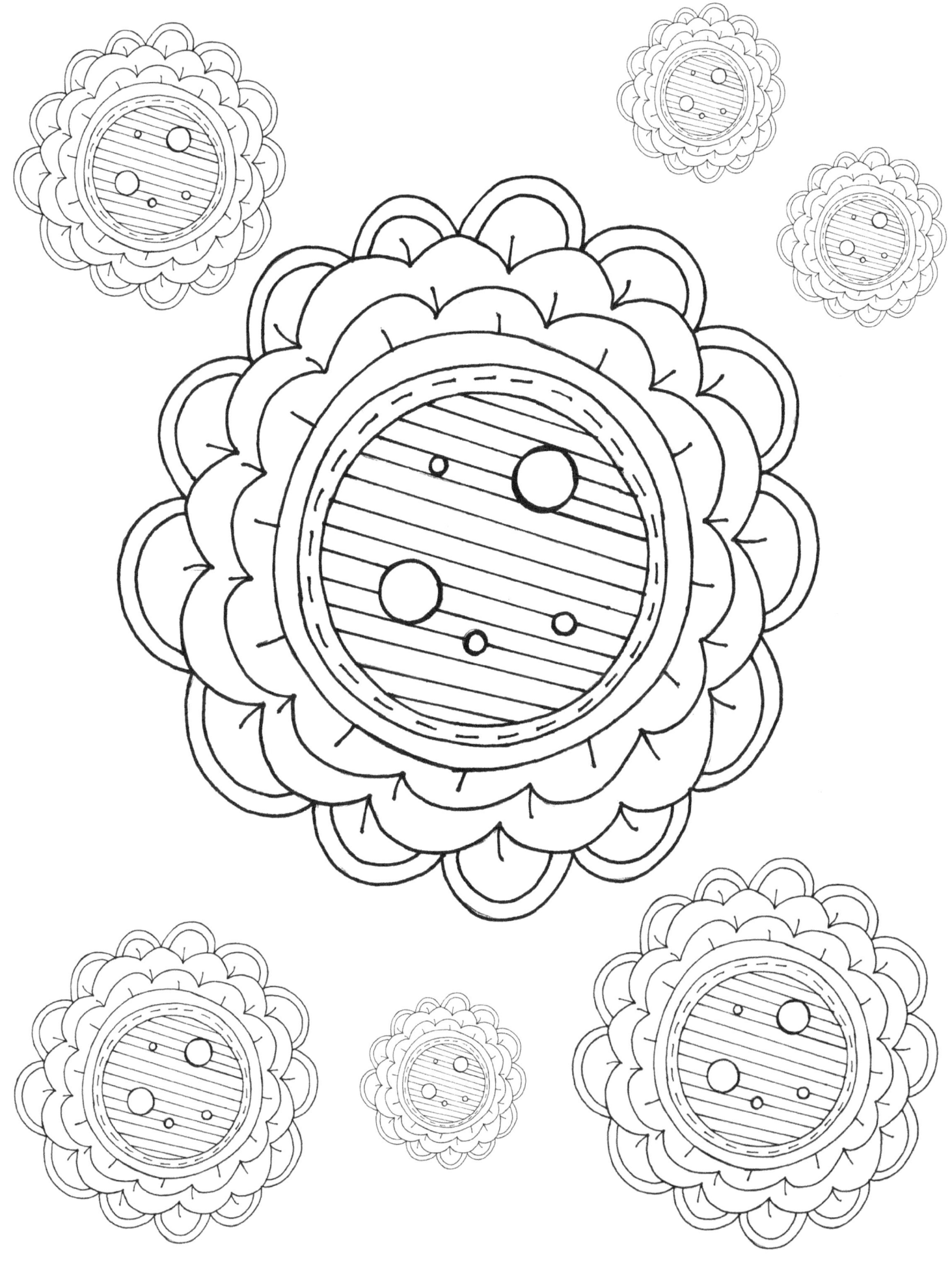

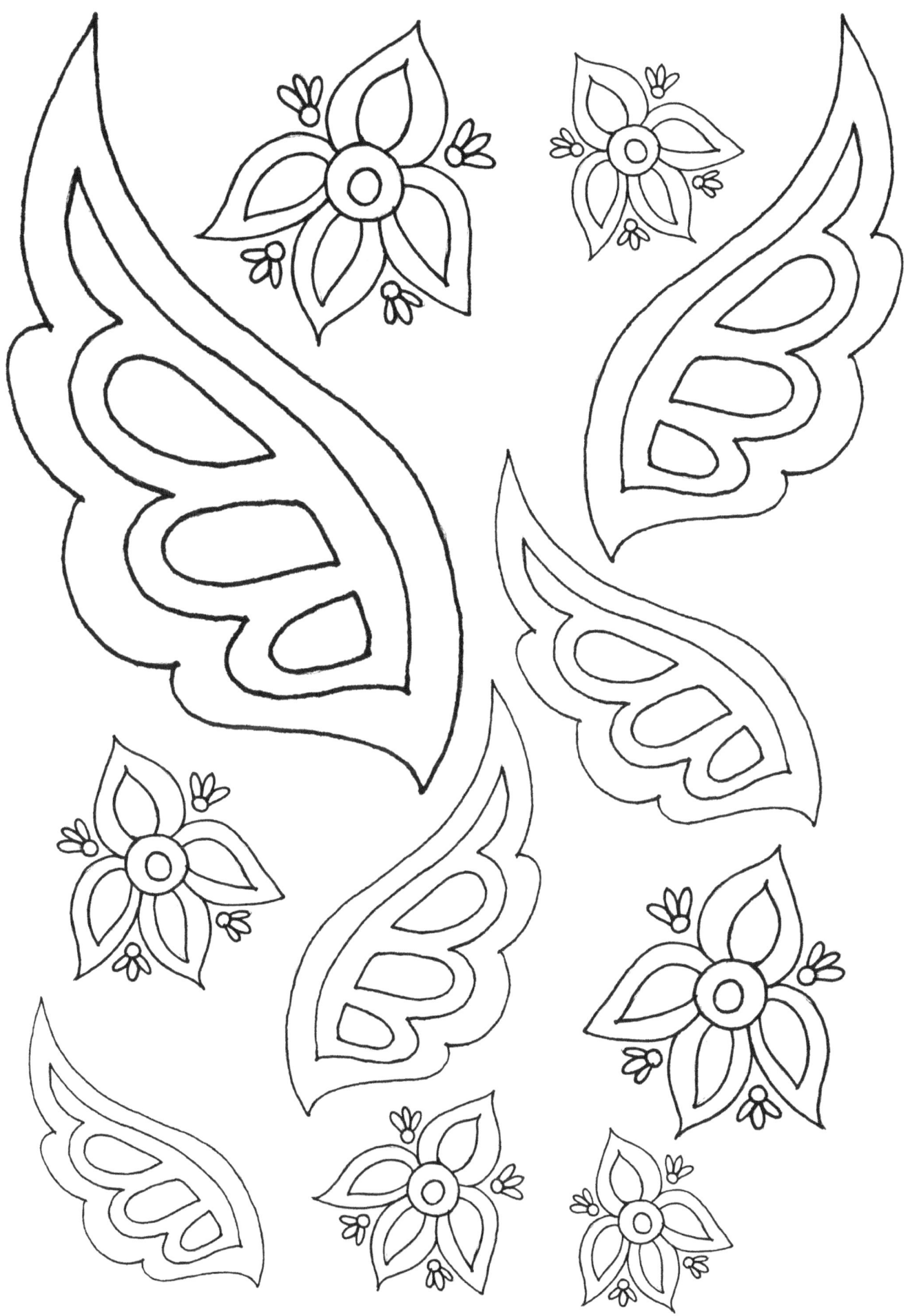

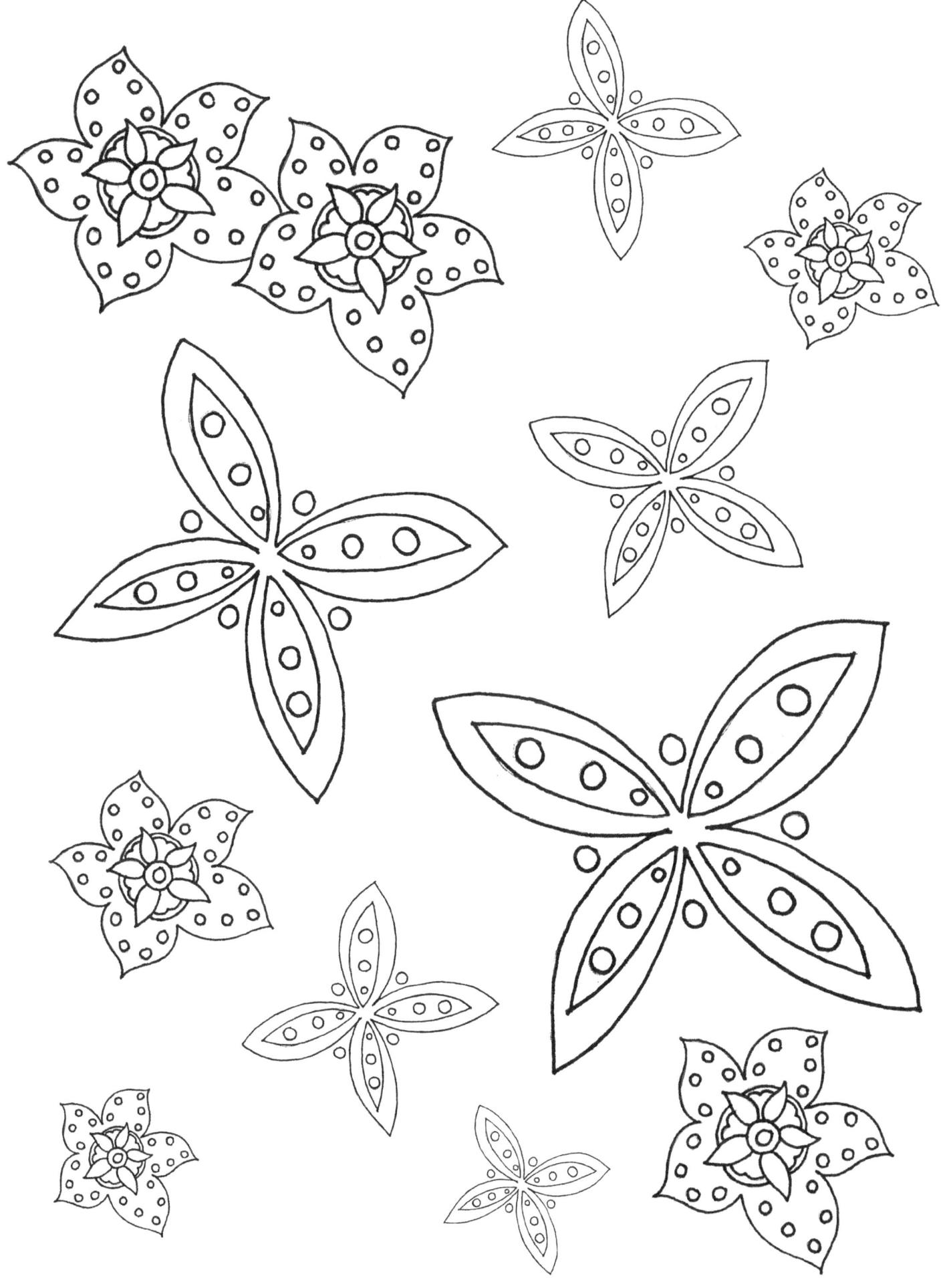

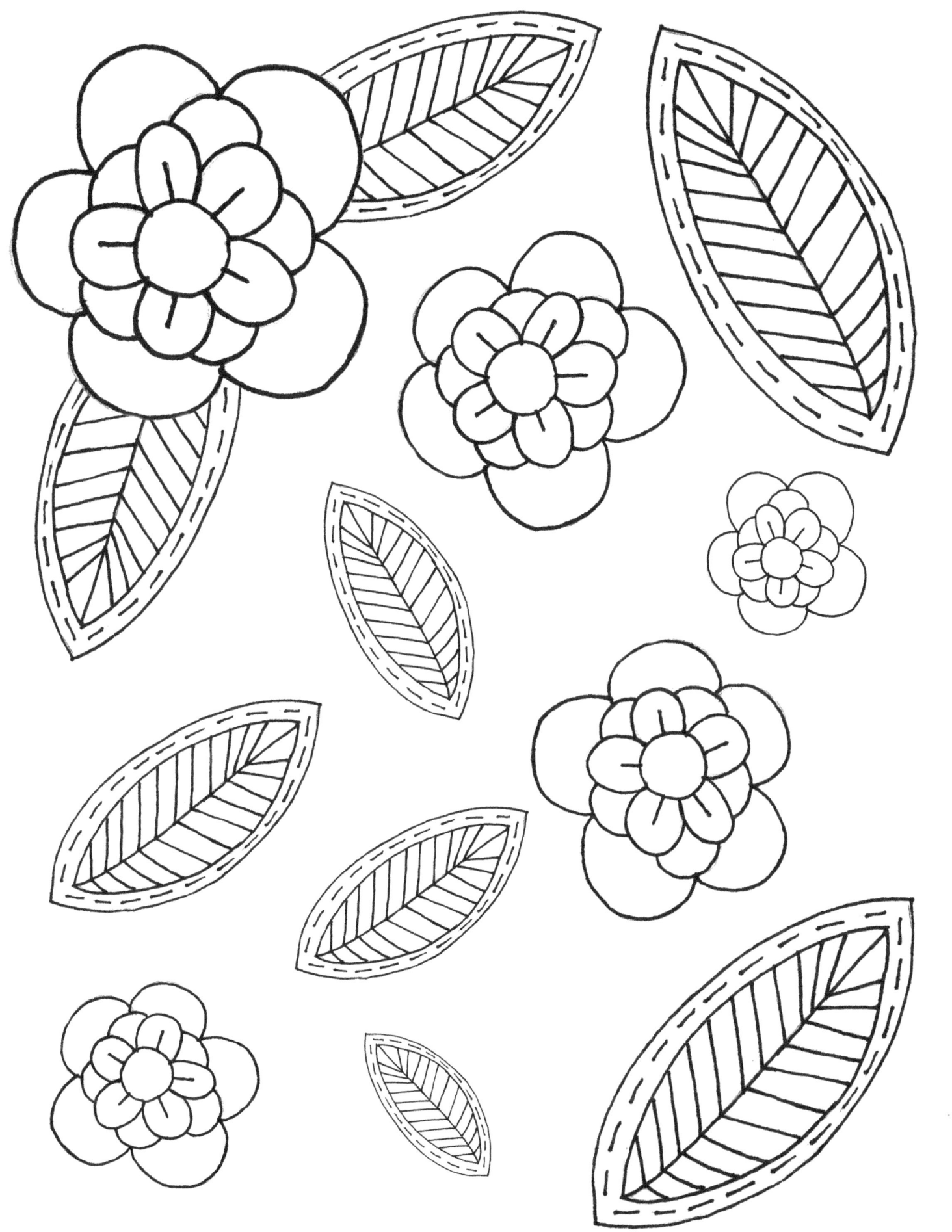

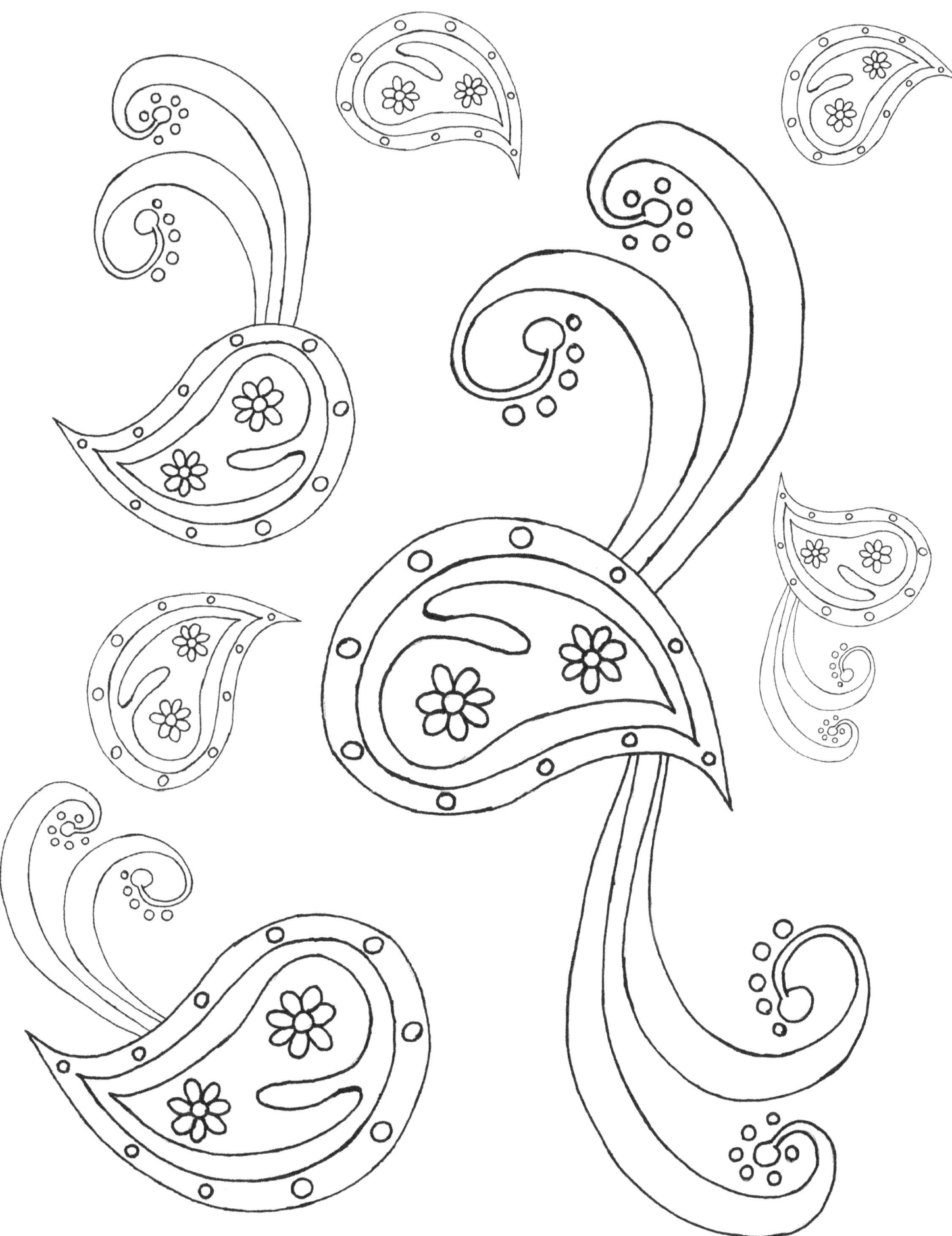

www.ingramcontent.com/pod-product-compliance
Lightning Source LLC
Chambersburg PA
CBHW080642190526
45169CB00009B/3471